Crabs and lobsters
all have **SHELLS**

and so does the turtle,
who lives in the sea.

Bears like to sleep in dark, warm **CAVES**,

where bats may hang,
upside down,
by their feet.

Some animals live in
NESTS in trees.
Birds do, when they
lay their eggs,

and so, in the evenings,
do chimpanzees.

High in the grass
the field mouse **NEST**
is a peaceful place to be

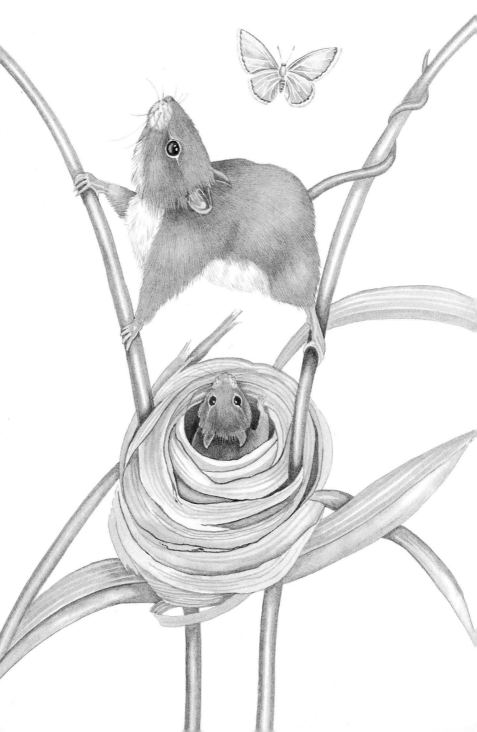

The busy **HIVE** of the honey bees hums and buzzes
with life.

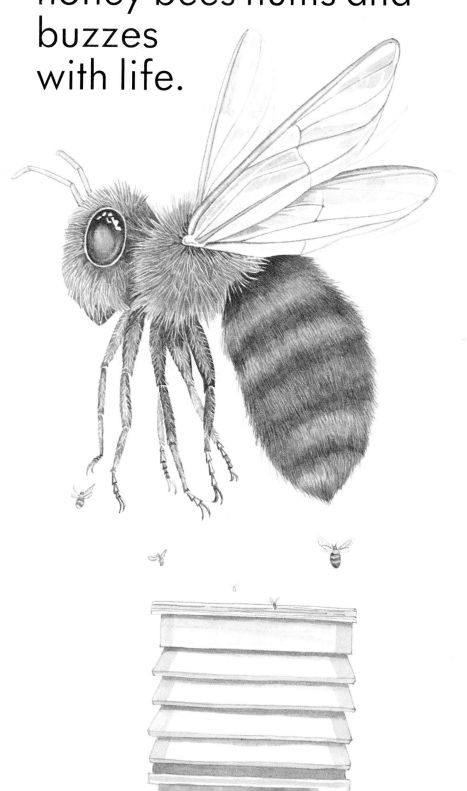

Rabbits and moles have homes underground.

They're safe and snug in their **BURROWS**.

The badger's home is called its **HOLE**,

while the fox curls up warm in its **DEN**.

A **WEB** is where a spider lives, spinning silk to catch its prey.

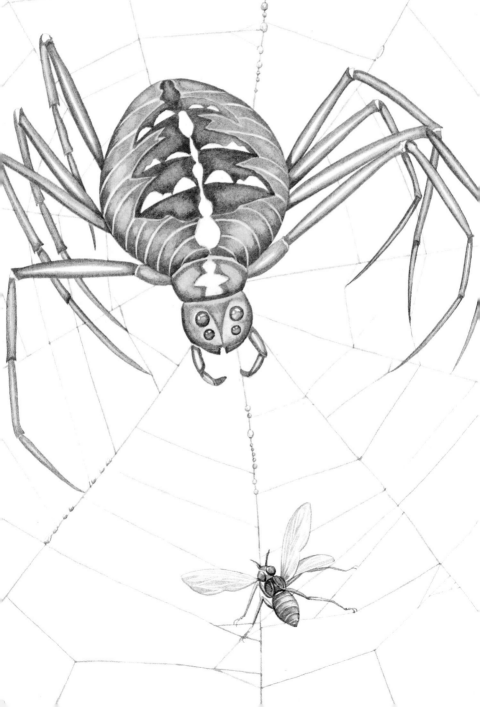

But the clever beaver
cuts down trees
to make a **LODGE**
its home.

Do you remember all their **HOMES**?